EL SALVADOR 2016 HUMAN RIGHTS REPORT

Note: This report was updated 4/12/17; see Appendix F: Errata for more information.

EXECUTIVE SUMMARY

El Salvador is a constitutional multiparty republic. Municipal and legislative elections held in March 2015 were generally free and fair. Election results were delayed, however, due to problems with the transmission, tabulation, and public dissemination of the vote count under the management of the Supreme Electoral Tribunal. Free and fair presidential elections took place in 2014.

Civilian authorities failed at times to maintain effective control over security forces.

The principal human rights problems stemmed from widespread extortion and other crime in poor communities throughout the country. They included widespread corruption; weak rule of law, which contributed to high levels of impunity and government abuse, including unlawful killings by security forces, discrimination, and delay and lack of compliance with court rulings; and violence against women and girls (including by gangs), gender discrimination, and commercial sexual exploitation of women and children. According to a 2016 CID Gallup poll, more than one in five families claim to have been victims of violent crimes.

Other human rights problems included harsh and potentially life-threatening prison conditions; lengthy pretrial detention; restrictions on freedom of speech and press; trafficking in persons; migrant smuggling, including of unaccompanied children; and discrimination against persons with disabilities and persons with HIV/AIDS. There was also widespread discrimination and some violence against lesbian, gay, bisexual, transgender, and intersex (LGBTI) persons.

Impunity persisted despite government steps to dismiss and prosecute some officials in the security forces, the executive branch, and the justice system who committed abuses.

Section 1. Respect for the Integrity of the Person, Including Freedom from:

a. Arbitrary Deprivation of Life and other Unlawful or Politically Motivated Killings

During the year there were no verified reports that the government or its agents committed politically motivated killings. There were reports, however, of security force involvement in unlawful killings. As of October the attorney general was investigating 53 possible cases of extrajudicial killings. One took place in 2013, none in 2014, 11 in 2015, and 41 in 2016. The Attorney General's Office also announced the formation of a Special Group Against Impunity, dedicated to investigating this type of crime. As of March the Office of the Human Rights Ombudsman (PDDH) had received 12 complaints of alleged unlawful killings committed by security, military, and other public officials and found substantial evidence in two cases. In September the PDDH stated that it was aware of approximately 50 cases involving potential extrajudicial killings. From January to July, the Office of the Inspector General of the National Civilian Police (PNC) reported that 12 PNC officers faced charges of homicide. All but one of the alleged homicides were committed while the accused officers were on duty.

On April 25, the PDDH found indications that the PNC and the armed forces had committed extrajudicial killings during the March 2015 San Blas case (involving the killing of seven alleged gang members and one other person) and the August 2015 Pajales case (which involved the close-range killing of four unarmed gang members). The PDDH criticized the PNC and the armed forces for issuing a press release portraying the killings as the product of clashes with gang members. The PDDH also noted weak internal controls in the PNC and the armed forces and regretted the lack of interagency collaboration in the investigations. On July 9, the attorney general ordered the arrest of seven police officers accused of committing extrajudicial killings in the San Blas case on charges of homicide and obstruction of justice. Seven officers were charged in the Pajales case, although there was no confirmation arrests were made.

On July 9, the Attorney General's Office ordered the arrest of five police officers and five civilians for their participation in at least eight homicides as part of an alleged extermination group operating in San Miguel; on July 13, a judge ordered preventive detention of the accused. Eleven additional defendants fled from justice, according to the Attorney General's Office. Funding for the extermination group reportedly came from Salvadorans living abroad.

The nongovernmental organization (NGO) Cristosal compared PNC data that showed 366 armed confrontations through July 2016, during which 350 suspected gang members died. A total of 359 suspected gang members were killed in 676 armed confrontations in 2015, and 83 were killed in 256 confrontations in 2014. The mortality rate of suspected gang members in confrontations with police during the first six months of the year was 109 percent higher (i.e., more than double) that the 2015 mortality rate, which was itself 41 percent higher than in 2014. On October 4, the digital newspaper *El Faro* cited a Brazilian expert who analyzed PNC data and concluded that the data demonstrated a pattern of abuse of lethal force by police authorities.

As of August, the Office of the Inspector General of the Ministry of Public Security and Justice had received two complaints of extrajudicial killings against police members and two complaints for violations to the right of life.

b. Disappearance

There were no reports of politically motivated disappearances, abductions, or kidnappings. As of September, the NGO Association for the Search for Missing Children (Pro-Busqueda) received five new complaints regarding children who disappeared during the 1980-92 civil war. Pro-Busqueda reported in August that it was investigating 960 open cases, had solved 425 cases, and determined that in 15 percent of solved cases the child had died.

According to the PNC inspector general, eight complaints of forced disappearances were filed against the PNC between January and August.

c. Torture and Other Cruel, Inhuman, or Degrading Treatment or Punishment

The law prohibits such practices, but there were multiple reports of violations. The PDDH received 21 complaints of torture or cruel, inhuman, or degrading treatment by the PNC, armed forces, and other public officials.

As of August, the Office of the Inspector General reported 31 complaints against police officers for alleged cruel treatment. The NGOs Foundation of Studies for the Application of the Law, and Passionist Social Service, as well as other civil society institutions reported that poor male youths were sometimes targeted by the PNC and armed forces because they fit the stereotype of gang members. Other credible sources indicated that youths suspected to have knowledge of gang activity were mistreated by law enforcement personnel.

NGOs reported that public officials, including police, engaged in violence and discrimination against sexual minorities. Persons from the LGBTI community stated that the agencies in charge of processing identification documents, the PNC, and the Attorney General's Office harassed transgender and gay individuals when they applied for identification cards or reported cases of violence against LGBTI persons. The LGBTI community reported authorities harassed LGBTI persons by conducting strip searches and questioning their gender in a degrading manner. The government responded to these abuses primarily through PDDH reports that publicized specific cases of violence and discrimination against sexual minorities.

Prison and Detention Center Conditions

Prison and detention center conditions remained harsh and life threatening due to gross overcrowding, unhygienic conditions, and gang activities.

Physical Conditions: Overcrowding remained a serious threat to prisoners' health and lives. As of August 15, the prison directorate reported 34,938 inmates were being held in correctional facilities with a designed capacity of 10,035 inmates. As of July 11, the minister of security noted that his office had moved 1,600 inmates from pretrial detention into the regular prison system. The Salvadoran Foundation for Economic and Social Development (FUSADES) estimated that, as of June 30, prison overcrowding was 346 percent. The prison population included 24,675 inmates with convictions and 10,263 inmates in pretrial detention. In many facilities, provisions for sanitation, potable water, ventilation, temperature control, medical care, and lighting were inadequate. On November 14, the PDDH published a report on deteriorating prison conditions, observed during fact-finding missions between April and July. The report highlights worsening conditions since the April implementation of extraordinary measures, including decreased access to medical care while infectious diseases increased, lack of sanitation facilities for the number of inmates, inmates sleeping on the floor without blankets, and inmates lacking space to sleep because of extreme overcrowding.

Men and women had separate accommodations within the prisons. A separate women's prison in Ilopango was generally clean and allowed inmates to move freely within and inmates' children under the age of five to stay with their mothers.

Due to prison overcrowding, police authorities held some pretrial detainees in small detention centers at police stations, which had a combined capacity of 2,102 persons. FUSADES reported in February that authorities held approximately 83 percent of these pretrial detainees in detention centers longer than the 72 hours legally permitted before presenting them to a court, some for up to two years. Similarly, due to the lack of holding cells, authorities often held pretrial detainees in regular prisons with violent criminals.

On March 16, the Legislative Assembly approved temporary provisions to allow parole for inmates considered low-level threats and with prison sentences of less than eight years (291 inmates).

On May 27, the Constitutional Chamber of the Supreme Court declared unconstitutional the systematic violation of basic human rights by prison overcrowding, citing the government for violating prisoners' right to health, and ordered periodic visits by the Ministry of Health. The court ordered prison authorities to build new prisons and to remodel others to shelter inmates humanely and the judicial system to review the inmate rosters with an aim of reducing the number of prisoners. Authorities closed one prison during the year, and another was under construction.

In November 2015 the Public Opinion Institute of the University of Central America (IUDOP-UCA) released the findings of its 2009-15 study on the penitentiary and prison system. The report estimated that 9 percent of the prison population was ill, including with highly communicable diseases such as tuberculosis. In August the General Directorate of Prisons (DGCP) began addressing tuberculosis within the prison system by creating mobile tuberculosis treatment teams and separate holding cells for infected inmates.

Prisoners conducted criminal activities from their cells, at times with the complicity of prison guards. Smuggling of weapons, drugs, and other contraband such as cell phones and cell-phone SIM cards was a major problem in the prisons. On April 1, the Legislative Assembly unanimously approved "extraordinary security measures" to prevent gang members from orchestrating crimes from within the prison system. These measures included preventing communication between inmate gang leaders and their members outside prison, suspending all private communication and contact with their families and limiting access to their lawyers, and detaining and isolating known gang leaders in higher security prisons. The measures also subjected the inmates in prisons designated for convicted gang members to isolation and restriction to their cells for 24 hours per day. According to the PDDH, prison authorities modified some of the measures in July and August and allowed prisoners up to one hour outside of their cells. The extraordinary measures affected 13,162 inmates housed in seven prisons: Izalco, Quezaltepeque, Chalatenango, Ciudad Barrios, Gotera, and Zacatecoluca penitentiaries, as well as one sector of Ilopango penitentiary. In response, approximately 200 relatives of imprisoned gang members organized a march on June 29 to demand the government reinstate family visits and file a complaint with the PDDH. On November 18, the government launched additional extraordinary measures in response to an increase in homicides of police officers and soldiers by gang members. These measures included moving gang members considered responsible for attacks against police officers to higher-security prisons and increasing their isolation.

Gang activities in prisons and juvenile holding facilities remained a serious problem. As of August 15, detention center facilities held 16,215 inmates who were current or former gang members. On October 22, the Prison Directorate ordered 235 inmates moved to different prisons in an effort to break up gang "cliques" within prisons. As of May, the Salvadoran Institute for Child Development (ISNA) reported that two adolescents died in juvenile detention facilities. ISNA also reported that there were 418 juveniles convicted and 230 juveniles awaiting trial.

According to news reports, 25 prisoners were killed within prisons between January and August, including 11 prisoners killed in the Gotera Penitentiary by fellow inmates. As of August, the Prison Directorate had reported only 11 homicides within prisons.

As of September 6, prison authorities removed two guards from duty for carrying illegal objects and sanctioned 29 guards for misconduct. Prison authorities received 17 complaints of human rights violations allegedly committed by prison personnel.

There was no information available regarding abuse of persons with disabilities in prisons, although the government's National Council for Comprehensive Attention to Persons with Disability (CONAIPD) previously reported isolated incidents, including sexual abuse.

Administration: The IUDOP-UCA report noted that, between 2009 and 2015, parole board staffing decreased by 48 percent. In 2015 the prison system had 69 technical employees (including attorneys, sociologists, social workers, and psychologists) to provide services to more than 31,000 inmates. The PDDH has authority to investigate credible allegations of inhuman conditions. The Constitutional Chamber of the Supreme Court has authority regarding the protection of constitutional rights.

<u>Independent Monitoring</u>: The government permitted prison-monitoring visits by independent human rights observers, NGOs, and the media, except to those prisons covered by the extraordinary measures. The PDDH continued to monitor all prisons. Church groups, the Central American University's Human Rights Institute, LGBTI activists, and other groups visited prisons during the year. After the implementation of the extraordinary measures, which restricted monitoring of the prisons subject to the measures, the International Committee for the Red Cross suspended all prison visits until visitation was restored in the prisons subject to the extraordinary measures.

d. Arbitrary Arrest or Detention

Although the constitution prohibits arbitrary arrest and detention, there were numerous complaints that the PNC and military forces arbitrarily arrested and detained persons. As of August, the Office of the Inspector General had received 45 complaints against police officers for alleged violations of freedom of movement. NGOs reported that the PNC had arbitrarily arrested and detained groups of persons on suspicion of gang affiliation. According to these NGOs, the accused were ostracized by their communities upon their return, even when they were not affiliated with gangs.

Role of the Police and Security Apparatus

The PNC, overseen by the Ministry of Justice and Public Security, is responsible for maintaining public security, and the Ministry of Defense has responsibility for maintaining national security. Although the constitution separates public security and military functions, it allows the president to use the armed forces "in exceptional circumstances" to maintain internal peace and public security "when all other measures have been exhausted." President Sanchez Ceren renewed the decree authorizing military involvement in police duties through the end of the year.

The three quick reaction military battalions that were created in 2015 to support PNC operations and whose troops have arrest and detention authority continued to operate. The military is responsible for securing the international border and conducting joint patrols with the PNC.

On April 20, the government announced the launch of the Fast Reaction Force (FERES), a joint operation consisting of two 200-officer police units supported by

250 Special Forces military soldiers. Battalion soldiers are legally able under citizen's arrest authority to detain persons they believe have committed criminal acts.

In response to an alleged rise in extrajudicial killings, the PNC in January launched a newly organized internal investigative office, the Secretariat for Professional Responsibility. The body is composed of a Complaints Office, a Disciplinary Office, and the Inspector General's Office.

From January to August, the Inspector General's Office received 492 complaints of human rights violations--31 for inhuman and cruel treatment, 181 for physical abuse, 117 for personal security, 40 for violence against women (including rape and sexual abuse), 15 for failure to provide access to justice, two for extrajudicial killing, and two for deprivation of life. The Inspector General's Office referred three of the cases to the Attorney General's Office for possible criminal charges.

In June the PDDH released its annual findings on the status of human rights. The report stated that, between June 2015 and May 2016, the PDDH received 1,883 complaints of human rights violations, 1,284 of which were reportedly committed by the PNC and the military.

Inadequate training, lack of enforcement of the administrative police career law, arbitrary promotions, insufficient government funding, failure to enforce evidentiary rules effectively, and instances of corruption and criminality limited the PNC's effectiveness. The PDDH has the authority to investigate (but not prosecute) human rights abuses and refers all cases it deems to involve human rights abuse to the Attorney General's Office.

In May PNC director Howard Cotto stated that since January 80 police officers had been arrested for illicit activities, such as extortion, theft, and murder for hire. In June the Inspector General's Office reported that it sanctioned 781 officers in response to complaints filed during the year and in prior years. These sanctions included 84 arrests and 165 officers suspended without pay. As of July 18, the Attorney General's Office reported that it had filed charges against 587 police officers and 14 judges for unspecified crimes. The office also reported that it successfully convicted 15 police officers for criminal activities.

The Inspector General's Office and the Ministry of Defense Human Rights Office reported most PNC officers, police academy cadets, and all military personnel had received human rights awareness training, including training by the Salvadoran

Institute for the Development of Women, the Human Rights Institute of the University of Central America, and the Inter-American Institute of Human Rights. The Inspector General's Office reported that 633 police officers received human rights training in the past year. The Ministry of Defense Human Rights Office reported that 6,097 soldiers received human rights training during the year.

On May 29, the PNC revised its guidelines on the use of force to improve accountability of police personnel. The guidelines specifically outline situations that permit the use of force, proportionality of force for various confrontational situations, and internal investigation procedures for alleged misconduct.

Arrest Procedures and Treatment of Detainees

The constitution requires a written warrant of arrest except in cases where an individual is in the act of committing a crime. Authorities apprehended persons with warrants based on evidence and issued by a duly authorized official. Police generally informed detainees promptly of charges against them.

The law permits release on bail for detainees who are unlikely to flee or whose release would not impede the investigation of the case. The bail system functioned adequately in most cases. The courts generally enforced a ruling that interrogation without the presence of counsel is coercive and that evidence obtained in such a manner is inadmissible. As a result, PNC authorities typically delayed questioning until a public defender or an attorney arrived. Detainees normally had access to counsel of their choice or to an attorney provided by the state. The constitution permits the PNC to hold suspects for 72 hours before presenting them to court, after which the judge may order detention for an additional 72 hours to determine if an investigation is warranted. The law allows up to six months for investigation of serious crimes before requiring either a trial or dismissal of the case. In exceptionally complicated cases, the prosecutor may ask an appeals court to extend the deadline for three or six months, depending on the seriousness of the crime. Many cases continued beyond the legally prescribed period.

Arbitrary Arrest: As of November 8, the PDDH reported 62 complaints of arbitrary detention or illegal detention during the year.

Pretrial Detention: Lengthy pretrial detention was a significant problem. As of June 30, 29 percent of the general prison population was in pretrial detention. Lengthy legal procedures, large numbers of detainees, judicial inefficiency, corruption, and staff shortages caused trial delays. Because it could take several years for a case to come to trial, some persons remained in pretrial detention longer than the maximum legal sentences for their alleged crimes. In such circumstances, detainees may request a Supreme Court review of their continued detention.

Detainee's Ability to Challenge Lawfulness of Detention before a Court: The constitution grants detainees the right to a prompt judicial determination on the legality of their detention, and persons arrested or detained may obtain prompt release and compensation if found to have been unlawfully detained. In some cases persons were not promptly released and/or did not receive compensation for unlawful detention.

e. Denial of Fair Public Trial

Although the constitution provides for an independent judiciary, the judiciary was burdened by inefficiency and corruption, and the Solicitor's Office (responsible for public defenders) of the Attorney General's Office and the PDDH suffered from insufficient resources. As of July 18, the Attorney General's Office reported that it had initiated 14,162 cases and obtained 3,268 convictions.

As of August, the Office of the Inspector General of the Ministry of Public Security and Justice reported 15 cases of violations of access to justice committed by police officers, and one police officer was accused of obstructing due process.

On July 13, the Constitutional Chamber of the Supreme Court struck down the 1993 Amnesty Law on the grounds that it violated citizens' constitutional right of access to justice and the right to compensation for crimes against humanity and war crimes. The law provided blanket protection against criminal prosecution and civil penalties for crimes committed during the country's civil war (1980-92), and the court's ruling held that the Legislative Assembly did not have authority to grant an absolute amnesty. Nevertheless, the court held that the law continues to be enforced for those crimes committed during the civil war years that do not constitute serious human rights abuses. The ruling declaring the Amnesty Law unconstitutional empowered parties to request judges to reopen cases related to civil war era crimes and for individuals to petition the attorney general to open new cases.

On August 25, the Supreme Court denied the extradition to Spain of former colonel Guillermo Benavides for the 1989 murder of four Jesuit priests. The court ordered Benavides to remain in prison to await a hearing before the Fourth Instruction Court of San Salvador to determine whether he would be held criminally responsible for the murders as a result of the Amnesty Law ruling. On September 30, in response to a petition by the victims, a judge issued an order to reopen the investigation into the 1981 El Mozote massacre, in which an estimated 800 persons were killed. On October 17, the Human Rights Institute at the University of Central America filed five complaints with the Attorney General's Office on behalf of victims of torture, forced disappearances, and murder from 1975 to 1989, allegedly by agents of the state. On October 20, Armando Duran filed a complaint against former Farabundo Marti Liberation Front (FMLN) commanders, including the sitting president, Salvador Sanchez Ceren, for their alleged participation in a kidnapping in 1987. On November 15, the Constitutional Court ordered a lower court judge to determine how to investigate and prosecute the 1982 "El Calabozo" massacre, in which approximately 200 persons were killed.

Substantial corruption in the judicial system contributed to a high level of impunity, undermining the rule of law and the public's respect for the judiciary. Between January 1 and June 30, the Supreme Court heard 201 cases against judges due to irregularities, removed four judges, suspended 10 others, and brought formal charges against 63 judges.

The Legislative Assembly did not always comply with Supreme Court rulings. As of September 8, the Legislative Assembly had not complied with a ruling from the Supreme Court's Constitutional Chamber that mandated the Legislative Assembly renominate magistrates on the Court of Accounts (a transparency oversight body) by July 29 because those nominated by the legislature had political party affiliations in contravention of legal standards. On September 6, the Constitutional Chamber of the Supreme Court admitted a complaint against the Legislative Assembly for failing to nominate members to the National Judicial Council after a delay of more than a year. The council is responsible for selecting judicial candidates.

Between January and June 20, the Ministry of Justice and Public Security's Executive Technical Unit (UTE), which provides witness protection services, provided protection to 682 victims, 821 witnesses, and 457 victim/witnesses. The unit also provided household protection for 55 persons. In 2015 the unit provided protection to 4,218 victims and witnesses. Some judges denied anonymity to witnesses at trial, and gang intimidation and violence against witnesses contributed to a climate of impunity from criminal prosecution.

Trial Procedures

The law provides for the right to a fair public trial, and an independent judiciary generally enforced this right, although some trial court judges were subject to political and economic influence. Although procedures called for juries to try certain crimes, including environmental pollution and certain misdemeanors, judges decided most cases. By law juries hear only a narrow group of cases, such as environmental complaints, to which the law does not assign to judges. After the jury's determination of innocence or guilt, a panel of judges decides the sentence in such cases.

Defendants have the right to be present in court, question witnesses, and present witnesses and evidence. The constitution further provides for the presumption of innocence, the right to be informed promptly and in detail of charges, the right to a trial without undue delay, protection from self-incrimination, the right to communicate with an attorney of choice, the right to adequate time and facilities to prepare a defense, freedom from coercion, the right to confront adverse witnesses and present one's own witnesses and evidence, the right to appeal, access for defendants and their attorneys to government-held evidence relevant to their cases, and government-provided legal counsel for the indigent. In criminal cases a judge may allow a private plaintiff to participate in trial proceedings (calling and cross-examining witnesses, providing evidence, etc.), assisting the prosecuting attorney in the trial procedure. Defendants have the right to free interpretation as necessary from the moment charged through the appeals process if the defendant does not understand Spanish. Authorities did not always respect these legal rights and protections. Although a jury's verdict is final, a judge's verdict is subject to appeal. Trials are public unless a judge seals a case. The law extends these rights to all citizens.

Political Prisoners and Detainees

There were no reports of political prisoners or detainees.

Civil Judicial Procedures and Remedies

The law provides for access to the courts, enabling litigants to bring civil lawsuits seeking damages for, as well as cessation of, human rights violations. Domestic court orders generally were enforced. Most attorneys pursued criminal prosecution and later requested civil compensation.

f. Arbitrary or Unlawful Interference with Privacy, Family, Home, or Correspondence

The constitution prohibits such actions, and there were no reports that the government failed to respect these prohibitions.

In many neighborhoods, armed groups and gangs targeted certain persons, interfered with privacy, family, and home life, and created a climate of fear that the authorities were not capable of restoring to normal.

Section 2. Respect for Civil Liberties, Including:

a. Freedom of Speech and Press

The constitution provides for freedom of speech and press, and the government generally respected these rights. Some restrictions, however, occurred throughout the year. The law permits the executive branch to use the emergency broadcasting service to take over all broadcast and cable networks temporarily to televise political programming.

Freedom of Speech: The constitution provides that all persons may freely express and disseminate their thoughts and that the exercise of this right is not subject to government censorship. Nevertheless, there were allegations that the government retaliated against individuals for criticizing government policy.

Credible sources indicated that the director of a transparency NGO, whose board of directors was composed of government officials, was removed from his position because he publicly criticized the government for what he viewed as "excessive and discretionary use" of classified information and because he demanded the government disclose "politically sensitive" information, such as financial data related to former president Funes' trips.

Violence and Harassment: On February 16, police arrested four suspects, including the communications director for the San Salvador mayor's office, in connection with a 2015 cyberattack against the website of the newspaper *La Prensa Grafica*.

On August 9, Minister of Defense Munguia Payes held a press conference, accompanied by other armed forces high commanders, to criticize "irresponsible" reporting by *La Prensa Grafica* following an article that cited irregularities in the

Ministry of Defense's account of lost firearms. On August 15, the vice president of the local chapter of the Inter-American Press Association alleged that the press conference was an attempt by Munguia Payes to intimidate the press and prevent media scrutiny of the Ministry of Defense. Munguia Payes was also accused of attempting to intimidate legislators when he attended a December 6 plenary session in the Legislative Assembly on lifting the immunity of a general accused of arms trafficking with three uniformed military officers; legislators ultimately lifted the immunity for General Jose Atilio Benitez.

ARENA Legislator Ricardo Velasquez forcefully grabbed a camera operator in an effort to move him from a Legislative Assembly entrance while verbally threatening the media on September 29, 2016. The legislator also filed a complaint against the camera operator's company for obstructing freedom of transit, which the Salvadoran Journalist Association (ANEP) labeled an "abuse of power" by the legislator.

On November 29, *La Prensa Grafica* journalist Cristian Melendez denounced threats that he received via Twitter from an account named "Sociedad Civil," suggesting that people "kill him" or "break his fingers if you see him on the street." He believed he received the threats in retaliation for his article alleging corruption involving San Salvador Mayor Nayib Bukele *La Prensa Grafica* had also published reports linking Bukele to a trolling case and cyberattacks against the newspaper.

Censorship or Content Restrictions: Government advertising accounted for a significant portion of press advertising income, although exact data was not publicly available. Newspaper editors and radio directors occasionally discouraged journalists from reporting on topics the owners or publishers might not view favorably. According to the Salvadoran Association of Journalists (APES), the media practiced self-censorship, especially in its reporting on gangs and narcotics trafficking.

In May the government censored a commercial advertisement that depicted various ways of living--including gay relationships, religious options, and public breastfeeding--and contained the tagline, "good is bad."

Journalist contacts reported experiencing threats from persons they believed to be government officials after reporting on the topic of violence in the country. They said these experiences diminished journalists' willingness to report on the security situation.

In December 2015 the PNC chief of police investigations, Joaquin Hernandez, filed a complaint against *El Diario de Hoy* newspaper after it published maps depicting areas that were controlled by gangs, citing law classifying gangs as terrorist organizations and charging the editor with advocating terrorism and inciting crimes, violations punishable by up to four years in prison. While the charges were not prosecuted, free press advocates cited the incident as an attempt to compel self-censorship by journalists.

Nongovernmental Impact: APES noted journalists reporting on gangs and narcotics trafficking were subject to threats and intimidation, which led to self-censorship.

Internet Freedom

The government did not restrict or disrupt access to the internet or censor online content, and there were no credible reports that the government monitored private online communications without appropriate legal authority. Internet access was available in public places throughout the country. The International Telecommunication Union reported 27 percent of the population used the internet during the year.

Academic Freedom and Cultural Events

After the July 9 Constitutional Chamber of the Supreme Court decision declaring alternate legislators unconstitutional, Constitutional Chamber judges faced increased difficulty in conducting outreach programs due to FMLN-organized protests. On August 13, protesters blocked Justice Florentin Melendez from reaching a venue to speak about constitutional rights to rural communities. As a result, on August 19, Justice Melendez announced that the Constitutional Chamber had decided to suspend its academic outreach program, "Know Your Constitution." On December 5, Melendez reported that constitutional justices had received death threats from protesters, whose signs included slogans such as, "death to the four constitutional judges." On December 8, the Attorney General stated that he was investigating the death threats against constitutional justices.

b. Freedom of Peaceful Assembly and Association

The constitution provides for the freedoms of assembly and association, and the government generally respected these rights, although there were occasions where the government used intimidation tactics to discourage assembly. On June 29, well-known LGBTI activist Bessy Rios was the single demonstrator in front of the President's Office, protesting a proposed increase in electricity prices, when the riot police arrested her, leaving bruises and scrapes on her body.

c. Freedom of Religion

See the Department of State's *International Religious Freedom Report* at www.state.gov/religiousfreedomreport/.

d. Freedom of Movement, Internally Displaced Persons, Protection of Refugees and Stateless Persons

The constitution provides for freedom of internal movement, foreign travel, emigration, and repatriation. The government generally respected these rights, although in many areas the government could not provide freedom of movement for any persons, due to the strength of criminal gang activity.

The government cooperated with the Office of the UN High Commissioner for Refugees (UNHCR) and other humanitarian organizations in providing protection and assistance to internally displaced persons, refugees, returning refugees, asylum seekers, stateless persons, and other persons of concern, but it was unable to facilitate services in many of the ungoverned neighborhoods most in need.

In-country Movement: Each gang had its own controlled territory. Gang members did not allow persons living in another gang's controlled area to enter their territory, even when travelling in public transportation. Gangs forced persons to present identification cards (that contain their addresses) to determine where they lived. If gang members discovered that a person lived in a rival gang's territory, that person might be killed, beaten, or not allowed to enter the territory. Bus companies paid extortion fees to operate within gang territories, often paying numerous fees for the different areas in which they operated. The extortion costs were passed on to paying customers.

Internally Displaced Persons

According to the most recent poll conducted in December 2014 by IUDOP-UCA, 4.6 percent of surveyed citizens reported being internally displaced due to violence and the threat of violence and 8 percent reported having tried to migrate to another country for the same reasons. In 2015 the NGO International Rescue Committee estimated that the number of displaced individuals was approximately 324,000, or 5.2 percent of the country's population.

In August the Civil Society Roundtable against Forced Displacement recorded cases of 623 displaced persons between August 2014 and December 2015 and an additional 396 displacements through August 2016; it determined that at least 86 percent of the displacements resulted from gang activity. Because these were documented cases from a group of NGOs with limited reach, actual displacement was likely much higher. Ministry of Education data showed that approximately 3,000 students dropped out of public schools in 2015 explicitly because of gang threats. Separate ministry data demonstrated that 15,511 students dropped out of all levels of public and private schools in 2015 because of crime and another 32,637 students left because they changed residence. NGOs suggested that changes in residence were often the result of forced displacement because of gang activity.

Protection of Refugees

Access to Asylum: The law provides for the granting of asylum or refugee status, and the government has established a system for providing protection to refugees. As of June 20, the government had granted refugee status to 10 individuals.

Section 3. Freedom to Participate in the Political Process

The constitution provides citizens the ability to choose their government in free and fair periodic elections held by secret ballot and based on universal and equal suffrage.

Elections and Political Participation

Recent Elections: The most recent municipal and legislative elections were held on March 1, 2015. The release of final election results by the Supreme Electoral Tribunal (TSE) electoral authorities was delayed until March 27, 2015, due to problems with the transmission, tabulation, and public dissemination of the vote count. International and domestic electoral observers participated in the election and counting process. The election report published by the Organization of American States electoral mission noted that, while the votes were being tabulated, "inconsistencies were discovered in a large number of records, due to erroneous data and information input by many voting centers."

In April 2015 the Constitutional Chamber of the Supreme Court ordered a vote-by-vote recount for the 24 legislators elected in the municipality of San Salvador, the country's largest constituency. The results of the recount did not alter any of the election results.

During the elections, as in the 2014 presidential elections, the Nationalist Republican Alliance (ARENA) and the FMLN political parties accused each other of fraud, including reports of double voting and voter intimidation.

On June 22, the Constitutional Chamber of the Supreme Court declared unconstitutional Article 195 of the electoral code, which prohibited police and soldiers from voting in polling stations where they provide security.

The law prohibits public officials from campaigning in elections, although this provision was not always enforced.

Participation of Women and Minorities: In 2013 the Legislative Assembly approved a law stipulating 30 percent of all candidates in municipal, legislative, and city council elections must be women. The law took effect during the March 2015 municipal and Legislative Assembly elections. There were 18 women in the 84-member Legislative Assembly, five women on the 15-member Supreme Court, and three women in the 13-member cabinet.

On October 18, newspapers reported that the TSE had taken action to advise a political party that its recent elections did not comply with the minimum quota and that it may need to substitute a woman for a man to comply with the law.

No members of the Supreme Court, the legislature, or other government entities identified themselves as members of an ethnic minority or indigenous community, and there were no political party positions or legislative seats designated for ethnic minorities.

Section 4. Corruption and Lack of Transparency in Government

The law provides criminal penalties for corruption by officials, but the government did not implement the law effectively. The NGO Social Initiative for Democracy stated that officials, particularly in the judicial system, often engaged in corrupt practices with impunity.

<u>Corruption</u>: Autonomous government institutions initiated several investigations into corruption. In late 2015 the Probity Section of the Supreme Court began, for the first time, to investigate seriously allegations of illicit enrichment of public officials. The Supreme Court reported that, as of July 22, the Probity Section investigated 72 current and former public officials for evidence of illicit enrichment and submitted five cases to the Attorney General's Office for possible criminal investigation. As of July 18, the Attorney General's Office reported investigating 93 cases related to corruption, resulting in seven convictions.

Attorney General Douglas Melendez, elected by the legislature in January, initiated criminal investigations of several public officials for corruption during the year. On June 6, the police arrested Apopa mayor Elias Hernandez on gang-related charges of illicit association, making threats, and aggravated homicide. On August 17, the Attorney General's Office executed search warrants on seven properties related to former president Mauricio Funes (2009-14) and opened a criminal corruption case against him. The government of Nicaragua granted Funes asylum on September 2. On August 22, police arrested former attorney general Luis Martinez and businessperson Enrique Rais on charges related to corruption. On October 30, former President Antonio "Tony" Saca (2004-09) was arrested on corruption-related charges, including embezzlement and money laundering, stemming from an alleged conspiracy to divert $18 million in government funds to private accounts. On November 5, a judge denied his bail.

<u>Financial Disclosure</u>: The illicit enrichment law requires appointed and elected officials to declare their assets to the Probity Section of the Supreme Court. The declarations are not available to the public, and the law does not establish sanctions for noncompliance. On May 12, the Supreme Court established three criteria for selecting which cases to investigate: the age of the case (i.e., proximity to the statute of limitations), the relevance of the position, and the seriousness and notoriety of the alleged illicit enrichment.

<u>Public Access to Information</u>: The law provides for the right of access to government information, but authorities did not always effectively implement the law. The law establishes mechanisms to appeal denials of information and report noncompliance with other aspects of the law. As of July, the Institute for Access to Public Information had formally received 1,001 cases, 81 percent of which had been resolved. The law gives a narrow list of exceptions that outline the grounds for nondisclosure and provide for a reasonably short timeline for the relevant authority to respond, no processing fees, and administrative sanctions for noncompliance.

Section 5. Governmental Attitude Regarding International and Nongovernmental Investigation of Alleged Violations of Human Rights

A variety of domestic and international human rights groups generally operated without government restriction, investigating and publishing their findings on human rights cases. Although government officials generally were cooperative and responsive to these groups, officials at times were reluctant to discuss certain issues, such as extrajudicial killings and the PDDH. The government required domestic and international NGOs to register, and some domestic NGOs reported that the government made the registration process unnecessarily difficult.

On January 28, the PNC launched the Secretariat for Professional Responsibility, which internally investigates all allegations of police misconduct.

<u>Government Human Rights Bodies</u>: The principal human rights investigative and monitoring body is the autonomous PDDH, whose head is nominated by the Legislative Assembly for a three-year term. The PDDH regularly issued reports and press releases on prominent human rights cases. The PDDH generally enjoyed government cooperation and was considered generally effective, except in areas controlled by criminal groups and gangs.

The PDDH maintained a constructive dialogue with the President's Office. The government publicly acknowledged receipt of PDDH reports, although in some cases it did not take action on PDDH recommendations, which are nonbinding.

On September 7, the deputy ombudsman stated the PDDH had inadequate resources to carry out the majority of its investigations.

The tenure of the ombudsman expired on August 8, by which time the Legislative Assembly was required to elect a new ombudsman. On September 22, the Legislative Assembly selected Raquel Caballero de Guevara as the new ombudswoman for a term of three years.

On October 26, anticipating the 25th anniversary of the peace accords, the PDDH created a consultative committee to define the role of the PDDH in the coming years. The committee was composed of civil society members representing legal, religious, environmental, economic, political, and health perspectives.

Section 6. Discrimination, Societal Abuses, and Trafficking in Persons

Women

Rape and Domestic Violence: The law criminalizes rape, and the criminal code's definition of rape may apply to spousal rape, at the judge's discretion. The law requires the Attorney General's Office to prosecute rape cases whether or not the victim presses charges, and the law does not permit the victim to withdraw the criminal charge. Cases may be dropped for lack of evidence if the victim refuses to provide it. The penalty for rape is generally six to 10 years' imprisonment, but the law provides for a maximum sentence of 20 years for raping certain classes of victims, including children and persons with disabilities.

Incidents of rape continued to be underreported for several reasons, including societal and cultural pressures on victims, fear of reprisal, ineffective and unsupportive responses by authorities to victims, fear of publicity, and a perception among victims that cases were unlikely to be prosecuted. Laws against rape were not effectively enforced.

Rape and other sexual crimes against women were widespread. On February 26, the PDDH criticized the Ministry of Justice and Public Security's UTE general director Mauricio Rodriquez, for failing to provide adequate security to seven female witnesses and victims of sex trafficking, one of whom was sexually assaulted by a security guard in a shelter supervised by the UTE. Although the victim filed a complaint, the security guard was not sanctioned or removed.

The Attorney General's Office reported that, as of July 18, 658 women had been victims of sexual-related crimes and 63 defendants had been convicted for sexual-related crimes against women. As of March 9, the Salvadoran Institute for the Development of Women (ISDEMU) reported 385 cases of rape against women.

ISDEMU provided health and psychological assistance to women who were victims of sexual abuse, domestic violence, mistreatment, sexual harassment, labor harassment, trafficking in persons, commercial sexual exploitation, or alien smuggling.

Violence against women, including domestic violence, was a widespread and serious problem. A large portion of the population considered domestic violence socially acceptable; as with rape, its incidence was underreported. The law prohibits domestic violence and generally provides for sentences ranging from one to three years in prison, although some forms of domestic violence carry higher penalties. The law also permits restraining orders against offenders. Laws against domestic violence were not well enforced, and cases were not effectively prosecuted. The law prohibits mediation in domestic violence disputes.

Between January and July 2016, ISDEMU reported 21 cases of femicide, 458 cases of physical abuse, 385 cases of sexual violence, and 2,259 cases of psychological abuse. ISDEMU reported 3,070 cases of domestic violence against women during the same period. In June ISDEMU issued its 2015 annual report on violence against women and reported that 230 died due to violence in the first six months of 2015, compared with 294 during the same period in 2014 and 217 in 2013.

ISDEMU coordinated with the judicial and executive branches and civil society groups to conduct public awareness campaigns against domestic violence and sexual abuse. The PDDH, the Attorney General's Office, the Supreme Court, the Public Defender's Office, and the PNC collaborated with NGOs and other organizations to combat violence against women through education, increased enforcement of the law, and programs for victims. The Secretariat of Social Inclusion, through ISDEMU, defined policies, programs, and projects on domestic violence and continued to maintain one shared telephone hotline and two separate shelters for victims of domestic abuse and child victims of commercial sexual exploitation. The government's efforts to combat domestic violence were minimally effective.

Women's rights NGOs claimed that many violent crimes against women occurred within the context of gang structures, where women were "corralled" and "disposed of at the whims of male gang members."

On March 3, women's rights activist for the NGO Hablame de Respeto ("Speak to me about respect") Aida Pineda was found dead, shot 11 times in front of her house in Milagrosa, San Miguel. Colleagues of Pineda contended that her killing was a femicide and that she was targeted for being a "powerful woman" who challenged the control of the Barrio 18 gang's repressive behavior toward women.

As of August, the Office of the Inspector General reported 40 cases of alleged violations of police officers against women due to their gender.

In an effort to sensitize the judicial system to gender-based violent crimes, the Legislative Assembly approved the creation of specialized courts for violence against women. The San Salvador courts began operations on June 1, while the San Miguel and Santa Ana courts were scheduled to start in 2017.

<u>Sexual Harassment</u>: The law prohibits sexual harassment and provides imprisonment of up to five years if the victim is an adult and up to eight years if the victim is a minor. Courts may impose fines in addition to a prison term in cases where the perpetrator is in a position of trust or authority over the victim. The law also mandates that employers take measures to avoid sexual harassment, violence against women, and other workplace harassment problems. The law requires employers to create and implement preventive programs to address violence against women, sexual abuse, and other psychosocial risks. The government, however, did not enforce sexual harassment laws effectively. Since underreporting by victims of sexual harassment appeared to be widespread, it was difficult to estimate the extent of the problem.

<u>Reproductive Rights</u>: Couples and individuals generally have the right to decide the number, spacing, and timing of having children; manage their reproductive health; and have access to the information and means to do so, free from discrimination, coercion, or violence. Access to reproductive health services outside of the capital city San Salvador, however, was limited.

Civil society advocates expressed concern that the country's complete abortion ban had led to the wrongful incarceration of women who suffered severe pregnancy complications, including miscarriages. Between 1999 and 2011, 17 women (referred to as "Las 17") were charged for having an abortion and convicted of homicide following obstetric emergencies and were sentenced to up to 40 years in prison. A petition was filed with the Inter-American Commission on Human Rights that highlighted violations of due process and of women's rights. Amnesty International and the UN Development Program claimed the women had miscarriages, while the Legal Medicine Institute argued that the women committed infanticide through abortion. In December 2014 one of "Las 17," Mirna Isabel Rodriguez, "Mima," was released after serving her prison sentence before her pardon could be finalized. On May 20, San Salvador's Third Tribunal Sentencing Court ruled there was not enough evidence to prove charges against a second member of the group, Maria Teresa Rivera, for aggravated homicide after having a miscarriage in 2011. On October 24, an appellate court did not admit a case against a third member, Santos Elizabeth Gamez Herrera. The Legislative Assembly was reviewing the remaining 14 cases. During the year the NGO Colectiva Feminista reported that two more women presented their cases, which included similarities with those of the "Las 17" women.

<u>Discrimination</u>: The constitution grants women and men the same legal rights but women did not enjoy equal treatment. The law establishes sentences of one to three years in prison for public officials who deny a person's civil rights based on gender and six months to two years for employers who discriminate against women in the workplace, but employees generally did not report such violations due to fear of employer reprisals.

Although pregnancy testing as a condition for employment is illegal, some businesses allegedly required female job applicants to present pregnancy test results, and some businesses illegally fired pregnant workers.

The law prohibits discrimination based on gender; nevertheless, women suffered from cultural, economic, and societal discrimination. The law requires equal pay for equal work, but according to the 2015 World Economic Forum Global Gender Gap Report, the average wage paid to women for comparable work was 60 percent of compensation paid to men. Men often received priority in job placement and promotions, and women did not receive equal treatment in traditionally male-dominated sectors, such as agriculture and business. Training was generally available for women only in low- and middle-wage occupations where women already held most positions, such as teaching, nursing, apparel assembly, home industry, and small business.

Children

<u>Birth Registration</u>: Children derive citizenship by birth within the country and from one's parents. The law requires parents to register a child within 15 days of birth or pay a $2.85 fine. While firm statistics were unavailable, many births were not registered. Failure to register resulted in denial of school enrollment.

<u>Education</u>: Education is free, universal, and compulsory through the ninth grade and nominally free through high school. Rural areas, however, frequently did not provide required education to all eligible students due to a lack of resources and because rural parents often withdrew their children from school by the sixth grade to allow them to work.

<u>Child Abuse</u>: Child abuse was a serious and widespread problem. Incidents of abuse continued to be underreported for a number of reasons, including societal and cultural pressures on victims, fear of reprisal against victims, ineffective and unsupportive responses by authorities toward victims, fear of publicity, and a

perception among victims that cases were unlikely to be prosecuted. During the year an appellate judge issued a report noting serious deficiencies in technical criteria for determining whether minors are victims of child abuse.

The Salvadoran Institute for the Comprehensive Development of Children and Adolescents (ISNA), an autonomous government entity, defined policies, programs, and projects on child abuse; maintained a shelter for child victims of abuse and female child victims of commercial sexual exploitation; and conducted a violence awareness campaign to combat child abuse. From January to May, ISNA reported providing psychological assistance to 131 children for physical and psychological abuse and 134 for sexual violence.

Early and Forced Marriage: The legal minimum age for marriage is 18, although the law authorizes marriage from the age of 14 if both the boy and girl have reached puberty, if the girl is pregnant, or if the couple has a child.

Sexual Exploitation of Children: Sexual exploitation of children, including girls and boys in prostitution, remained a problem. Child sex trafficking is prohibited by law, which prescribes penalties of 10 to 14 years' imprisonment for trafficking crimes. An offense committed against a child is treated as an aggravating circumstance, and the penalty increases by one-third, but the government did not effectively enforce these laws.

The minimum age for consensual sex is 18. The law classifies statutory rape as sexual relations with anyone under the age of 18 and includes penalties of four to 13 years' imprisonment.

The law prohibits paying anyone under the age of 18 for sexual services. The Secretariat of Social Inclusion, through ISDEMU, continued to maintain one shared telephone hotline for child victims of commercial sexual exploitation and victims of domestic abuse. The law prohibits participating in, facilitating, or purchasing materials containing child pornography and provides for prison sentences of up to 16 years for violations.

Displaced Children: Surveys indicated the primary motivations for migration were family reunification, a lack of economic and educational opportunity in the country, and fear of violence.

International Child Abductions: The country is a party to the 1980 Hague Convention on the Civil Aspects of International Child Abduction. See the

Department of State's *Annual Report on International Parental Child Abduction* at travel.state.gov/content/childabduction/en/legal/compliance.html.

Anti-Semitism

The Jewish community totaled approximately 150 persons. There were no known reports of anti-Semitic acts.

Trafficking in Persons

See the Department of State's *Trafficking in Persons Report* at www.state.gov/j/tip/rls/tiprpt/.

Persons with Disabilities

The law prohibits discrimination against persons with physical, sensory, intellectual, and mental disabilities in employment, education, air travel and other transportation, access to health care, and the provision of other state services. The National Council for Comprehensive Attention to Persons with Disability (CONAIPD), composed of representatives from multiple government entities, is the government agency responsible for protecting disability rights, but it lacked enforcement power. According to CONAIPD, the government did not allocate sufficient resources to enforce prohibitions against discrimination effectively, particularly in education, employment, and transportation. The government did not effectively enforce legal requirements for access to buildings, information, and communications for persons with disabilities. There were almost no access ramps or provisions for the mobility of persons with disabilities. Children with disabilities generally attended primary school, but attendance at higher levels was more dependent on their parents' financial resources.

According to CONAIPD, only 5 percent of businesses and nongovernment agencies fulfilled the legal requirement of hiring one person with disabilities for every 25 hires. There was no information available regarding abuse in educational or mental health facilities, although CONAIPD previously reported isolated incidents, including sexual abuse, in those facilities.

CONAIPD reported employers frequently fired persons who acquired disabilities and would not consider persons with disabilities for work for which they qualified. Some schools would not accept children with disabilities due to a lack of facilities and resources. There was no formal system for filing a discrimination complaint involving a disability with the government.

Due to their use of sign language, several young deaf individuals were confused with gang members (who also used signs to communicate) by police officers and soldiers and suffered mistreatment.

On May 25, CONAIPD and the Cooperative Transport Association Ciudad Delgado launched 10 bus units with platform access for persons with disabilities.

Several public and private organizations, including the Telethon Foundation for Disabled Rehabilitation and the National Institute for Comprehensive Rehabilitation (ISRI), promoted the rights of persons with disabilities. The Rehabilitation Foundation, in cooperation with ISRI, continued to operate a treatment center for persons with disabilities. CONAIPD reported that the government provided minimal funding for ISRI.

Indigenous People

A 2014 constitutional amendment recognizes the rights of indigenous people, but no laws provide indigenous people rights to share in revenue from exploitation of natural resources on historically indigenous lands. The government did not demarcate any lands as belonging to indigenous communities. Because few possessed title to land, opportunities for bank loans and other forms of credit were extremely limited.

During the year the municipalities of Conchagua and Santo Domingo de Guzman, which have relatively higher populations of Nahuat speakers, approved regulations to improve the living conditions for women, persons with disabilities, and older indigenous individuals in the towns and made reference to their historic lands.

Acts of Violence, Discrimination, and Other Societal Abuses Based on Sexual Orientation and Gender Identity

Although the law prohibits discrimination on the basis of sexual orientation and gender identity, discrimination against LGBTI persons was widespread, including in employment and access to health care. In May the PDDH conducted a survey of transgender individuals and reported that 52 percent had suffered death threats or violence, of which 23.7 percent had reported the incidents.

NGOs reported that public officials, including police, engaged in violence and discrimination against LGBTI persons. Members of the LGBTI community stated that PNC and Attorney General's Office personnel ridiculed them when they applied for identification cards or reported cases of violence against LGBTI persons. The NGO Space for Lesbian Women for Diversity claimed that, as of November, the Attorney General's Office had not prosecuted any cases of killings and other violent acts or of possible human rights violations committed by public officials against LGBTI persons. The Secretariat for Social Inclusion reported that 11 LGBTI persons were killed during the year because of their sexual orientation. The PDDH reported that since 2009 a total of 18 LGBTI persons were killed because of their sexual orientation.

Wilber Leonel Flores Lopez, a former soldier, was charged with attempted murder of a transgender individual on April 9. Flores was arrested on August 23. On August 26, an initial hearing was held in the First Court of Peace of Santa Ana, where the testimony of the victim, medical reports, and other forensic evidence were analyzed. The judge, however, did not order prison detention for Flores. The trial was pending, and prosecutors appealed the judge's decision not to jail Flores.

On May 30, the newspaper *La Prensa Grafica* reported that police had uncovered the body of a transgender woman who had been beaten and strangled to death. An autopsy report by the Forensic Science Institute showed that the victim's body was mutilated and showed indications that the victim was sexually violated. The PNC did not declare a motive for the killing. LGBTI NGOs alleged the victim was targeted due to her transgender identity and that authorities refused to investigate the crime from that angle.

On August 10, the Attorney General's Office pressed assault charges against five officers involved in the assault in January 2015 of Alex Pena, a transgender man and municipal police officer. On October 6, police officers Melvin Neftali, Hernandez Alvarado, and Francisco Balmore Hernandez were convicted and sentenced to four years in prison for assault. The other officers were acquitted. On October 6, the government reported on the convictions using Pena's female birth name.

HIV and AIDS Social Stigma

Although the law prohibits discrimination on the basis of HIV/AIDS status, Entre Amigos, a LGBTI NGO, reported that discrimination due to HIV was widespread. Lack of public information and medical resources, fear of reprisal, fear of ostracism, and mild penalties incommensurate with the seriousness of the discrimination remained problems in confronting discrimination against persons with HIV/AIDS or in assisting persons suffering from HIV/AIDS. As of June 30, the PDDH reported four cases of discrimination against persons with HIV or AIDS. As of October, the Ministry of Labor had reported one case of discrimination against an HIV-positive employee based on the illness.

Section 7. Worker Rights

a. Freedom of Association and the Right to Collective Bargaining

The law provides the right of most workers to form and join independent unions, to strike, and to bargain collectively. The law also prohibits antiunion discrimination, although it does not require reinstatement of workers fired for union activity. Several restrictions limit these rights. Military personnel, national police, judges, and high-level public officers may not form or join unions. Workers who are representatives of the employer or in "positions of trust" also may not serve on the union's board of directors. The law does not define the term "positions of trust." The labor code does not cover public sector workers and municipal workers, whose wages and terms of employment are regulated by the 1961 civil service law. The constitution guarantees the formation of associations by employees but prohibits police, military, and certain judicial sector employees from forming either a union or a formal association.

Unions must meet complex requirements to register legally and to have the right to bargain collectively, including a minimum membership of 35 workers. If the Ministry of Labor denies a union's legal registration, the law prohibits any attempt by the union to organize for up to six months following the denial. Collective bargaining is obligatory only if the union represents the majority of workers.

While workers have the right to strike, the law contains cumbersome and complex registration procedures for conducting a legal strike. The law does not recognize the right to strike for public and municipal employees or for workers in essential services, which include those services where disruption would jeopardize or endanger life, security, health, or normal conditions of existence for some or all of the population. The law does not specify which services meet this definition, and courts therefore apply this provision on a case-by-case basis. The law places several other restrictions on the right to strike, including the requirement that 30 percent of all workers in an enterprise must support a strike for it to be legal and that 51 percent must support the strike before all workers are bound by the decision to strike. In addition, unions may strike only to obtain or modify a collective bargaining agreement or to protect the common professional interests of the workers. They must also engage in negotiation, mediation, and arbitration processes before striking, although many groups often skipped or went through these steps quickly. The law prohibits workers from appealing a government decision declaring a strike illegal.

The Labor Court ruled 10 strikes illegal. These rulings covered the strikes of the following unions: the Social Security Institute strike in May, the Bloom Hospital strike in July, the Nurses' Union strike in November, the Health Labor Union strike in November, and the Ministry of Economy strike in November. They also covered the strikes of the Bloom, San Bartlo, Zacamil, Nueva Guadalupe, Sensuntepeque, La Union, Jiquilisco, Usulutan, Ciudad Barrios, and Sonsonate hospitals, which, during a national labor reduction, demanded enforcement of a salary step increase as provided by law. No arrests were made during the strikes. During the hospital strikes, there were reports of intervention by activists and one legislator of the governing party.

In lieu of requiring employers to reinstate illegally dismissed workers, the law requires employers to pay them the equivalent of 30 days of their basic salary for each year of service completed, plus the corresponding proportion for any partial year. This compensation must never be less than 15 days of basic salary. The law specifies 30 reasons for which an employer can legally terminate a worker's contract without triggering any additional responsibilities on the part of the employer. Such reasons include consistent negligence by an employee, leaking of private company information, or committing immoral acts while on duty. Short of terminating workers, an employer may also legally suspend workers in a variety of situations, including for reasons of economic downturn or market conditions. As of June, the Ministry of Labor had encountered 339 cases of unpaid salary in the course of 11,065 inspections of employers.

The government did not effectively enforce the laws on freedom of association and the right to collective bargaining in all cases. Resources to conduct inspections were inadequate, and remedies remained ineffective. Penalties for employers who disrupt the right of a union to exist by directly or indirectly firing workers with the goal or effect of ensuring the union no longer met the minimum number of members ranged from 10 to 28 times the monthly minimum salary. The maximum penalty for employers who interfere with the right to strike was $114. Such penalties were generally not sufficient to deter violations. The Ministry of Labor acknowledged it lacked sufficient resources, such as vehicles, fuel, and computers, to enforce the law fully. Judicial procedures were subject to lengthy delays and appeals. According to union representatives, the government did not consistently enforce labor rights for public workers, maquila/textile workers, subcontracted workers in the construction industry, security guards, informal sector workers, and migrant workers. As of June, the Ministry of Labor had received five claims of violation of the freedom of association.

As of June, the Ministry of Labor imposed 181 fines on businesses and individuals for workplace violations. The ministry received 3,325 complaints of illegal firing and ordered 115 workers to be returned to work. Although not required by law, the ministry continued to request that some employers rehire fired workers, basing its requests on International Labor Organization (ILO) Administrative Court rulings. The ministry did not perform inspections in the informal sector. News reports indicated that 66 percent of the economically active population worked in the informal economy. According to the 2015 census, 42 percent of all workers in urban areas worked in the informal sector. The ministry does not have jurisdiction over public employees, most of whom are under the civil service law.

Workers faced problems exercising their rights to freedom of association and collective bargaining, including, according to allegations by some unions, government influence on union activities and antiunion discrimination on the part of employers. Unions were independent of the government and political parties, although many generally were aligned with ARENA, the FMLN, or other political parties.

There were reports of antiunion discrimination, including threats against labor union members, dismissals of workers attempting to unionize, and blacklisting. Workers at times engaged in strikes regardless of whether the strikes met legal requirements.

b. Prohibition of Forced or Compulsory Labor

The law prohibits all forms of forced or compulsory labor. The government generally did not effectively enforce such laws. Resources to conduct inspections were inadequate. The labor code allows penalties for violations of up to 28 times the minimum monthly wage, which was generally not sufficient to deter violations. The lack of sufficient resources for inspectors reduced their ability to enforce the law fully. There were no reports of forced labor, according to the Ministry of Labor. Gangs subjected children to forced labor in illicit activities, including selling or transporting drugs (see section 7.c.).

Also see the Department of State's *Trafficking in Persons Report* at
www.state.gov/j/tip/rls/tiprpt/.

c. Prohibition of Child Labor and Minimum Age for Employment

The law prohibits the employment of children under the age of 14. The law allows
children between the ages of 14 and 18 to engage in light work if the work does not
damage the child's health or development or interfere with compulsory education.
The law prohibits children under the age of 16 from working more than six hours
per day and 34 hours per week; those under the age of 18 are prohibited from
working at night or in occupations considered hazardous. The Ministry of Labor
maintained a list of the types of work considered hazardous and prohibited for
children, which include repairing heavy machinery; mining; handling weapons;
fishing and harvesting mollusks; and working at heights above five feet while
doing construction, erecting antennas, and working on billboards. Children who
are 16 and older may engage in light work on coffee and sugar plantations and in
the fishing industry so long as it does not harm their health or interfere with their
education.

The Ministry of Labor is responsible for enforcing child labor laws but did so with
limited effectiveness. The law specifies a default fine of no more than $60 for
each violation of most labor laws, including child labor laws; such penalties were
insufficient to act as a deterrent. The ministry's labor inspectors focused almost
exclusively on the formal sector. As of June, the ministry reported that it had
conducted 511 inspections related to child labor during which inspectors reported
two incidents of child labor and three incidents of adolescents working without
permits. There was no information on any investigations or prosecutions by the
government. The ministry lacked adequate resources for effective enforcement of
child labor laws in the agricultural sector, especially in coffee and sugarcane
production, or in the large informal sector.

The government continued to participate in an ILO project to provide educational
opportunities to children while offering livelihood alternatives for their families.
Through this project the Ministry of Education promoted child labor awareness and
encouraged school attendance, including operating after-school programs in 2,000
schools during the year. The ILO project concluded in March. During the year the
ministry developed a permanent work plan for child labor verification aimed at
eliminating the worst forms of child labor and creating a culture of compliance and
respect for the law among employers.

Child labor remained a serious and widespread problem. According to the *2015 Permanent Household Survey* published in 2016, there were approximately 140,700 child workers (between the ages of five and 17). The worst forms of child labor occurred in coffee and sugarcane cultivation, fishing, mollusk shucking, and fireworks production. In order to survive, orphans and children from poor families frequently worked as street vendors and general laborers in small businesses. Children also worked as domestic servants and endured long work hours and abuse by employers. Children were subjected to commercial sexual exploitation (see section 6, Children) and were recruited into illegal gangs to perform illicit activities related to the arms and drug trades, including committing homicide.

Also see the Department of Labor's *Findings on the Worst Forms of Child Labor* at www.dol.gov/ilab/reports/child-labor/findings/.

d. Discrimination with Respect to Employment and Occupation

The constitution, labor law, and regulations prohibit discrimination regarding race, color, sex, religion, political opinion, national extraction (except in cases determined to protect local workers), social origin, gender, disability, language, or HIV-positive status. The government did not effectively enforce those laws and regulations. Sexual orientation and gender identity are not included in the constitution, although the PDDH and Ministry of Labor actively sought to protect workers against discrimination on those grounds.

Discrimination in employment and occupation occurred with respect to gender, disability, and sexual orientation and/or gender identity (see sections 6 and 7.e.). According to the Ministry of Labor, migrant workers have the same rights as citizens, but the ministry did not enforce them.

e. Acceptable Conditions of Work

There is no national minimum wage; the minimum wage is determined by sector. According to the Ministry of Labor, the minimum daily wage was $8.39 for retail and service employees, $8.22 for industrial laborers, and $7.03 for apparel assembly workers. The agricultural minimum wage was $3.94 per day. The government reported that the poverty income level was $179.67 per month in urban areas and $126.97 in rural areas.

The law sets a maximum normal workweek of 44 hours, limited to no more than six days and to no more than eight hours per day, but allows overtime if a bonus is paid. The law mandates that full-time employees receive pay for an eight-hour day of rest in addition to the 44-hour normal workweek. The law provides that employers must pay double-time for work on designated annual holidays, a Christmas bonus based on the time of service of the employee, and 15 days of paid annual leave. The law prohibits compulsory overtime. The law states that domestic employees are obligated to work on holidays if their employer makes this request, but they are entitled to double pay in these instances. The government did not adequately enforce these laws.

The Ministry of Labor is responsible for setting workplace safety standards, and the law establishes a tripartite committee to review the standards. The law requires all employers to take steps to ensure that the health and safety of employees are not at risk in the workplace. To provide for the health and safety of workers, the law requires employers to take preventive safety measures, including providing proper equipment and training and a violence-free environment. Employers who violate most labor laws can receive a default fine of no more than $57 for each violation. For serious infractions employers can be fined up to an amount equivalent to 28 minimum monthly wage salaries. These penalties were insufficient to deter violations, and some companies reportedly found it more cost effective to pay the fines rather than comply with the law. The law promotes occupational safety awareness, training, and worker participation in occupational health and safety matters.

As of July 18, the Attorney General's Office reported that it had received 379 complaints against employers for not paying pension quotas to the pension administration companies and that it filed judicial charges against 82 employers. The judiciary dismissed charges in 48 cases and suggested alternative solutions in 46 cases.

The Ministry of Labor is responsible for enforcing the law. The government was more effective in enforcing the minimum wage law in the formal sector than in the informal sector. Unions reported that the ministry failed to enforce the law for subcontracted workers hired for public reconstruction contracts. The government provided its inspectors updated training in both occupational safety and labor standards. As of June, the ministry's 183 inspectors had conducted 11,065 inspections. Allegations of corruption among labor inspectors continued.

The ministry received complaints regarding failure to pay overtime, minimum wage violations, unpaid salaries, and cases of employers illegally withholding benefits (including social security and pension funds) from workers.

There were reports of overtime and wage violations in several sectors. According to the ministry, employers in the agriculture sector did not generally grant annual bonuses, vacation days, or days of rest. Women in domestic service and the industrial manufacturing sector for export industry, particularly in the export processing zones, faced exploitation, mistreatment, verbal abuse, threats, sexual harassment, and generally poor work conditions. Workers in the construction industry and domestic service were reportedly subject to violations of wage, hour, and safety laws. There were also reports of occupational safety and health violations in other sectors. The government was ineffective in pursuing such violations.

In some cases the country's high crime rate negatively affected acceptable conditions of work as well as workers' psychological and physical health. Some workers, such as bus drivers, bill collectors, messengers, and teachers in high-risk areas, reported being subject to extortion and death threats.

As of June, the Ministry of Labor reported 4,189 workplace accidents. The sectors registering the highest levels of incidents were the following: 1,822 accidents in the services sector, 1,435 in the industry sector, 484 in the commerce sector, 315 in the government sector, 67 in the municipal sector, 47 in the agricultural sector, and 19 in autonomous entities. The ministry did not report any deaths from workplace-related accidents.

Workers can legally remove themselves from situations that endanger health or safety without jeopardy to their employment, but authorities lacked the ability to protect employees in this situation effectively.